I0786789

A Program for a Modern Communist Party
Ricardo Santiago

2018 (c) Free People's Movement Archive

A Program for a Modern Communist Party

Ricardo Santiago

TABLE OF CONTENTS

Preamble

Regroup, reforge the international revolutionary movement!

Brothers, sisters, comrades:

The revolution is what matters. All of the old questions over which we have become so divided must take a back seat to the question of how to make revolution today – not in the interests of unity for unity's sake, but in the interests of eliminating the scourge of capitalism once and for all.

No one would deny – and in fact we are the first to point out – that all sorts of traitors, sell-outs, reformists and misleaders – conscious or not – have risen among the ranks of those calling themselves revolutionaries over the years, especially with our increased fractionalization. Rather than include such undesirable "comrades" in any reorganization of forces, we must expose and exclude them, for rather than strengthen our forces, they can only serve to confuse, misdirect and weaken them.

On this, all genuine revolutionaries can agree: we must liquidate the capitalists as a class, thus paving the way for the working class to take over and transform society. It is around this that we must unite.

We must organize ourselves as an international body, capable of attacking the global capitalist system at its weakest points, thus weakening its strongest points at the same time. It is with this in mind that a modern communist party must be formed. We urge you to engage our politics, look over our organizational, political and theoretical documents, and ultimately, to join us.

The Modern Communist Party

The modern communist party is not yet another sect declaring allegiance to this or that doctrine, but rather a force which bases itself on the living -- and constantly developing -- scientific communist theory first developed by Karl Marx and Friedrich Engels. The party's theoretical roots lie in our synthesis of the world communist movement, from its origins to today, formulated through a thorough analysis of its failures and successes.

The modern communist party's outlook is summed up by a statement made by Thomas Sankara, a leader of the 1983 revolution in Burkino Faso, who, along with Karl Marx, Friedrich Engels, V.I. Lenin, Rosa Luxemburg and Ernesto 'Che' Guevara stands among the party's political forebears:

> "We are open to all the winds of the will of the peoples and their revolutions, and we study some of the terrible failures that have given rise to tragic violations of human rights. We take from each revolution only its kernel of purity, which forbids us to become slaves to the reality of others."

The primary reason for the existence of the modern communist party is to facilitate, as *The Communist Manifesto* put it, "the forcible overthrow of all existing social conditions," by acting as the most advanced and resolute part of the working class. The organization of our party, and indeed our methods of work, are completely subordinated to this historic task.

Organization, Guidelines, and Methods of Work of the Modern Communist Party

Forward

1. Since the development of agriculture brought about an end to thousands of years of primitive society all of human history has been marked by the struggle between the classes that rule and the classes they rule over.

2. The means by which one class maintains its rule over the other classes is through the state–the organized forces of repression (military, police, courts, prisons, etc.).

3. All progressive leaps from one form of society to another have come as the result of the victory of one of the classes which were ruled over the class which ruled them -- processes which were themselves made possible by leaps in the mode of production (i.e. the method through which things are produced, for example by hand, with simple machines or with complex machines).

4. In the first form of class society -- slave society -- which was based on the use of animals in advanced agriculture, an aristocracy, usually claiming to be the incarnation or descendants of god or gods on earth, ruled over plebeians and slaves. That form of society was replaced by feudalism, which was based on the use of simple machines like the hand-mill, and

under which a different type of aristocracy ruled over the craftsmen and peasantry. That form of society has since been replaced by capitalism, which arose with the industrial revolution (i.e. when the hand-powered machines of feudalism were replaced with steam powered machines).

5. Capitalism -- the system which first emerged in Europe, and today prevails in the overwhelming majority of countries on earth -- has not done away with class divisions and class struggles. Instead, it has created a new class of rulers and new classes which are ruled over. Along with these new classes and class relations -- which are much more simplified than those of past epochs -- has come new forms of struggle.

6. The capitalist system is based on the exploitation of the toiling majority at the bottom of society (i.e. the working class, or proletariat) by, and for the benefit of, the exploiting minority at the top (i.e. the capitalist class, or bourgeoisie).

Thus the main antagonism, or division, in capitalist society exists between the capitalists, who control the means of production (i.e. the tools and technology used to produce the things human beings want and need, such as mines, factories, etc.) but don't work them, and the proletarians, who work the means of production but don't control them.

In much smaller numbers than the proletariat exists a "middle class," the petit-bourgeoisie -- made up of small shop keepers, managers, etc. -- whose individual members strive to join the capitalist class, but are constantly being thrown down into the working class by the very workings of capitalism.

Another class, the lumpenproletariat, or 'dangerous class' -- consisting of swindlers, pimps, hustlers, etc. -- constitutes an even smaller portion of society under capitalism. While sections of the lumpenproletariat may ally with the working class at one time or another, its conditions of life, greed and desperation make it more likely to side with the capitalists during open class conflict.

7. Under capitalism working people are wage-slaves. Lacking control of the means of production, they must sell their labor to the capitalist bosses or starve.

The capitalists, to whom workers are nothing more than another commodity, make their profits through the purchase of this labor at prices well below its value.

A simple example of this is a worker who assembles simply toys in a capitalist's factory for $5 an hour. The toys themselves are made by combining two plastic pieces, which the capitalist purchases for $1 each. The worker assembles ten toys an hour, so the capitalist has put forward $25 to create 10 new toys. The capitalist then sells the ten completed toys for $3 each, thus bringing in $30. Since the materials the toys were made of cost the capitalist $20, and the hour of labor of the worker cost him $5, he made a profit of $5. That profit came from the exploitation of the worker! The twenty plastic pieces alone were only worth $20. It was the labor of the worker that added value to those pieces, allowing them to be resold for an additional $10. But instead of receiving the full value she created ($10), the worker only receives a fraction ($5), and the parasitic capitalist keeps the rest. Now the worker who created 10 toys in an hour can only afford to buy 1 of them with the wages she received for an hour of work.

This is how capitalism functions; and this is the role of the working class -- the class that creates all wealth, but receives only enough of it in return to stay alive and continue producing workers -- which makes it the only truly revolutionary class.

8. Under capitalism, working people become alienated from their social relationships with one another through the way they

interact.

A worker who uses her pay to buy a hat made by another worker in a retail store doesn't see the relationship between herself and the other worker. Instead she sees only the relationship between the money and the hat -- something which appears to her to be independent of the people involved.

9. Through the early development of capitalism, as the factories replaced the craftsman's workshops, work began to require less and less special skill. Because of this, more and more people were drawn into the process of production, including women, and young and old men, who had previously been excluded. As the masses of workers came together in their different workplaces, under their respective bosses, their shared interests and conditions of life became more obvious to them. As these workers came into open conflict with their bosses over wages, job-security and the like, they began to form labor unions as organizations through which they could unite and use their collective power to defend their basic interests.

But unions were, as they remain, only basic organizations that are limited to the economic realm. Different forms of organization are necessary to wage a struggle in the political realm.

As well, labor unions are prone to becoming, and largely have come to be, dominated by bureaucrats who are separated from the workers they supposedly represent, and who sell them out at any opportunity to get a few more crumbs for themselves from the capitalist bosses.

10. While all previous revolutionary movements (e.g. the bourgeois revolutions that ushered in capitalism) were movements of minorities who sought to better their own social standing, the working class movement is a movement of the immense majority which seeks to abolish social standing all

together.

11. To break the unity of the working class, the capitalist class has historically relied on the age old tactic of "divide-and-conquer."

Through their control of the media (radio, television, newspapers, etc.), the education system, "scientific" studies and the like, the capitalists constantly promote as many "differences" between working people -- such as racial and national divisions -- as they can.

All of these "divisions" lack any basis in fact. "Race," for example, doesn't even exist (biologically speaking).

Instead, these divisions are social constructs, created by the rulers for the explicit purpose of keeping working people fighting among themselves (e.g. by giving workers from one race slightly more crumbs than another), in order to prevent them from fighting their real class enemies.

Further, the capitalist class excludes a certain number of workers from employment at all times. These workers, who make up the "army of the unemployed," are often used by the capitalist rulers as a battering ram against employed workers who take action around a set of demands.

In some capitalist countries prison inmates, subject to the wills of the wardens and guards who rule over them, can be included in this "army."

Because of their desperation (or, in the case of prison inmates, the threat of further punishment), the "army of the unemployed" is often eager to replace a higher paid workers for less pay, break a strike, or carry out some other similar action. The capitalist promotes this not only to keep down wages, but also to cause divisions and rifts in the working class as a whole.

12. Communism emerged as the expression of the interests of the working class and its historic task to abolish capitalism and

create a communist world, that is, a moneyless world free from national and class divisions, repression, exploitation, etc., in which the means of production are controlled collectively, and used to meet human need.

The working class cannot simply take control of this capitalist state and use it for its own purposes. Instead, the working class must destroy the capitalist state through socialist revolution and construct a proletarian state in its place.

Only the force of the proletarian state can successfully intervene in, and direct the relations of, the economy. Through this intervention and direction, management of production and distribution can be put under the control of the working class, and society can be reorganized to meet human needs.

Under the proletarian state, remaining elements of the capitalist class that do not integrate into the working class are denied all political rights and functions.

The proletarian state itself defends itself by taking all means of agitation out of the hands of counterrevolutionary elements, arming and organizing the working class to repulse all internal and external attacks, and fighting to extend the revolution to the remaining capitalist countries.

The transformation of the world economy and, consequently, social life -- made possible through international socialist revolution -- will lead to the disappearance of class antagonisms and the withering away of the workers' state. It is as that point that communist society will emerge.

13. Communists are those workers conscious of the historic task of their class. They do not operate independently of the working class, but rather work to raise the consciousness of their class brothers and sisters in order to facilitate the organization of the proletariat as a class and the overthrow of capitalism.

14. As the countries which first reached capitalism rapidly developed, their need for raw materials (e.g. coal, nickel, oil, etc.), cheap labor and new markets to sell their goods in grew as well. When they could no longer find these things in the quantities they required within their own borders, they began to look elsewhere. It was then that colonialism (i.e. the forceful seizure of areas, and often even people) was born.

Around the same time that most of the world outside of the capitalist powers became colonized, the capitalists found a need to invest a portion of the profits they acquired from the exploitation of the workers in their countries in other places. This need was based on the search for the cheapest labor, which could be found in the colonies (workers in the capitalist powers had already begun to gain class consciousness and organize, and weren't willing to work for such a small percentage of the value they created), and raw materials. This was the birth of imperialism -- the economic exploitation and domination of the imperialist-oppressed (so-called Third World) countries by the strongest capitalist countries (i.e. the imperialist powers).

Today, the imperialist powers are the United States, United Kingdom, Germany, Spain, France, Japan, Australia, Portugal, the Netherlands, Canada, Italy and Belgium. These countries are ruled by the most powerful capitalists on earth. The imperialists in the United States are presently particularly strong.

The imperialists do anything and everything they can, from staging coups to waging all out wars, to ensure their dominance over the colonies and neocolonies (i.e. officially "independent" countries which are still economically dominated by one of the various imperialist powers) they control.

Through their dominance, the imperialists are able to extract "super-profits" (i.e. much higher than average profits, accumulated through the super-exploitation of workers, for example, in sweatshops) from the imperialist-oppressed countries.

Through this process, the imperialists have, to a certain extent, been able to limit the recessions inherent to capitalism in their countries, though by no means have they been able to eliminate them.

The imperialists also use the consumer goods produced in the imperialist-oppressed countries to placate the workers in their own countries. The imperialists spread consumerism -- a preoccupation with acquiring more and more things -- to take the workers' minds off of their exploitation (workers with a car, stereo, television, etc. are usually much less likely to revolt than those who live in a shack with no electricity). Through these actions, the imperialists largely, but not entirely, transferred the conflict between the haves and have-nots from their own countries to the world stage. Even still, there is marked class contradiction in the imperialist countries themselves, and that contradiction can only increase as the imperialists attempt to roll back all of the gains that working people in their countries have made (e.g. higher wages, benefits, shorter working hours, etc.) through hard fought struggles.

Through their actions the imperialists have wrecked, and limited the development of large parts of the world, while centralizing wealth in their own countries. This has driven large numbers of working people to immigrate to the imperialist countries in search of a means of survival. The imperialists keep these immigrant workers in the position of second-class citizens, so that they can be paid less and used to foster divisions in the working class.

The imperialists pursue their own interests. Their every act is guided by their drive to conquer a larger part of the world and secure a bigger piece of the pie for themselves. All wars between the imperialists (e.g. World War I) and between imperialist powers and imperialist-oppressed countries (e.g. the current war in Iraq) have resulted from this drive.

The imperialists cannot be "forced" by any "peace movement," no matter how large, to end or limit their warmongering.

Only socialist revolution can smash imperialism.

15. Imperialism is a world system, and it must be defeated in a world confrontation.

Because of imperialist-oppression and super-exploitation, the main stage for socialist revolution today is in the imperialist-oppressed countries. As these countries are able to break free from imperialist domination -- by carrying out socialist revolutions -- the imperialist system itself will weaken, thus eliminating the very base on which imperialism relies, and bringing the imperialist countries themselves closer to socialist revolution.

In the first imperialist-oppressed countries in which the revolution breaks out, the struggle will be the most difficult. But with each victory, as increasing parts of earth are wrested from the hands of the capitalists, the realization of the ultimate goal of a communist world will become more attainable.

16. Owing to the rise of capitalism in some countries before others, imperialism, etc., the various countries of the world are each at different stages of development. Because of this, and because contradictions sharpen and ease (or appear to) at different times and in different conditions, revolutions occur within one country or another, rather than simultaneously across all borders.

Still, each of these revolutions has an international effect, as every country belongs to the world economy created by capitalism.

17. Since the earliest years of capitalism, working people have attempted -- in various geographic locations and to varying

degrees of success -- to overthrow their exploiters.

In 1871, a revolutionary uprising in Paris, France, created the Paris Commune, considered the first attempt at establishing a proletarian state.

The first successful attempt at overthrowing capitalism came in 1917, when the October Revolution sent shock waves through the world by overthrowing capitalist rule throughout the vast Russian Empire and laying the foundation for the Union of Soviet Socialist Republics (USSR).

The October Revolution, which was carried out by the proletariat – under the leadership of its Bolshevik party – destroyed the capitalist state and paved the way for the construction of a proletarian state in its place. Due to the USSR's backwardness, isolation, imperialist encirclement, the failure of the socialist revolution to successfully spread to other (especially more advanced) countries, and the loss of many of its most advanced members of the working class in the civil war, the revolution began to degenerate after a few years, giving rise to a privileged bureaucratic caste that eventually seized political power, thus making the USSR a bureaucratized proletarian state.

The bureaucracy did not own the means of production, which were brought into public ownership in the wake of the October Revolution, thus it was not a class. The bureaucracy was a conservative, nationalist caste that controlled the state.

18. After the October Revolution, capitalist rule was overthrown, and capitalist property relations subsequently overturned, in Mongolia, China, Viet Nam, Laos, Albania, Yugoslavia, Ethiopia, and the northern half of Korea. But the methods in which capitalism was overthrown in these countries gave rise not to healthy proletarian states, but bureaucratized proletarian states like that which existed in the USSR.

The bureaucrats who controlled these states came from

various backgrounds. Some were communists who had genuine revolutionary intentions but viewed "actually existing socialism" in the bureaucratized proletarian states that has already come into existence as the model for socialism and/or looked to the leaders of bureaucratized-socialist states (especially the USSR), who nationalistically subjected the interests of the international working class as a whole to the interests of their own countries, for leadership and direction. Others were opportunists, looking for a way to "get ahead." Finally, some were professional, administrators, et. al., in the old society seeking privileged positions for themselves in the new society.

In the states liberated from fascism by the Red Army during World War II (Bulgaria, Czechoslovakia, Hungary, Poland, Romania, and east Germany), the soon-to-be bureaucrats were placed a top bureaucratic states constructed by the Red Army on the model of the Soviet state.

In the states created through mass revolutions (China, Viet Nam, Laos, Albania, Yugoslavia, Mongolia, Ethiopia and north Korea), the soon-to-be bureaucrats insured the creation of bureaucratic proletarian states by patterning themselves on the bureaucratic castes that ruled the existing bureaucratized proletarian states.

19. While relying on its existence for their positions, the bureaucrats simultaneously undermine the bureaucratized proletarian state by pursuing their own narrow interests (especially by seeking out ways to get more privileges and to secure wealth and positions of power that can be inherited by their offspring).

The tendency of the bureaucracies to attempt to "peacefully coexist" with imperialism, allow increasing capitalist penetration into the economy and seek out new property forms, combined with the pressures of a hostile capitalist world, can lead to an eventual collapse of the bureaucratized proletarian state under the weight of its own contradictions. In the wake of such a collapse the bureaucracy will split, with the largest section most likely going over the internal and external forces of capitalist counterrevolution which will take full advantage of the situation to take power and forge a capitalist state. This is what occurred in the USSR, Mongolia, Yugoslavia, Albania, Bulgaria, Czechoslovakia, Hungary, Poland, Romania, and east Germany.

But this is not the only danger. The bureaucracy, along the proletarian state itself, cant be directly overthrown by counterrevolutionary forces, as was the case in Ethiopia.

20. Today, bureaucratized proletarian states remain in existence in China, Laos, Viet Nam and north Korea. All four are in serious danger of collapse, counterrevolution and capitalist restoration. If successful, such counterrevolution would represent a set back for the working class as a whole.

While bureaucratized proletarian states are a far cry from the proletarian states we fight for, they still represent a gain for the working class. Despite their distortions, the bureaucratic proletarian states exist over top of collectivized property form born out of the overthrow of capitalism, thus allowing working people much better living conditions than they had prior to (or in the cases of those which no longer exist) after the states' existence. More importantly on a historic scale, the very existence of these states contributes to the defeat of world imperialism, thus removing all barriers for the construction of genuine socialism in every country and paving the way for a communist world.

Communists fight for the establishment of genuine socialism in the bureaucratic socialist states, but they do not do so in a way which weakens those countries in the face of imperialist aggression or emboldens or assists counterrevolutionary elements. We struggle for the ouster of the bureaucrats and their governing system, to be replaced by genuine workers' democracy, while pointing out the need for the preservation of the gains represented by collectivized property, economic planning, and control of trade.

The best way for the working class to defend the gains in these countries is to defend the countries themselves from attack by the imperialist powers while at the same time fighting for socialist revolutions in the remaining capitalist countries. The victory of socialist revolutions in the capitalist countries can create the openings necessary for the removal of the bureaucratic castes in the bureaucratized proletarian states (e.g. by revitalizing the working class internationally, reducing the ability of the bureaucracies to prop their rule by pointing to the need to defend the country from the imperialists, etc.).

21. Other than the working class in the USSR, the working class of Cuba is so far the only in history to carry out socialist revolution (in 1959), take power, and hold on to it by establishing a healthy proletarian state. Today, Cuba is the only healthy proletarian state in existence. Still, revolutionary Cuba is in danger. It is a testament to the Cuban workers' internationalism and commitment to the revolution that the limited bureaucracy that exists in Cuba has been kept in check and prevented from taking power. If Cuba is not broken out of isolation by the victory of the socialist revolution in other countries, it will eventually degenerate under the harsh pressures it faces.

22. The initial outcome of mass democratic, national liberation and/or anti-capitalist revolutions in backward and imperialist-oppressed countries is often, but not always, the creation of an infant proletarian and farmers state, resting on top of the old capitalist economy. Such a state cannot hold out for long. The

revolution must either "grow over" into a socialist one (i.e. the toilers must mobilize and utilize their newly found state power as an instrument to expropriate the exploiters, establish a monopoly on foreign trade, reorganize the economy to meet human need, and consolidate the creation of the proletarian state) at a relatively quick pace, or be overthrown.

As the communist revolutionary Ernesto 'Che' Guevara pointed out, "...the indigenous bourgeoisies have lost all capacity to oppose imperialism – if they ever had any – and are only dragged along behind it like a caboose. There are no other alternatives. Either a socialist revolution or a caricature of revolution."

The revolutions in Nicaragua, Grenada, Burkino Faso and Afghanistan all gave birth to proletarian and farmers states which were subsequently overthrown.

23. Throughout the existence of capitalism, and especially since the October Revolution, numerous movements -- revolutionary and non -- have been lead or hijacked midstream by forces who -- like the bureaucracies in the bureaucratic socialist states they looked to -- claimed to be socialist or even "communist" to boost their credibility and/or authority (while violating every communist principle and acting against the interests of the working class).

The capitalists point to several of these instances (e.g. Cambodia) as real examples of communist theory in practice to discredit it. But just as every force claiming to be "democratic" is not, neither is/was every force claiming to be socialist or communist.

24. The various defeats of the working class have served to educate it. They have not ended its struggle.

Various bourgeois revolutions were defeated and turned

back before the ultimate victory of capitalism over feudalism on a world scale. Likewise, the inability of the working class to achieve absolute victory in the first waves of its revolutions have not eliminated its historic task, or the possibility and necessity of achieving it.

Contrary to the claims of the capitalists' mouthpieces who so boldly proclaim "the death of communism," the class struggle is again sharpening, and a new wave of revolutions -- made stronger through the lessons learned -- is approaching.

25. The prevailing outlook in any society is that of its ruling class. Under capitalism, this remains the case.

Through its control of the media, education systems, etc., the capitalists imbue working people with an outlook that runs counter to their interests. Working people are told from birth that there is no alternative to capitalism, that what's good for the capitalist bosses is good for everyone, that everyone can get ahead if they just work hard enough, that having more than others is the most important thing, and often even that there is no way to know what is true and what isn't.

As well, the capitalists create the myth of "national unity" between all people in each country. This is done, along with a concerted effort, and often even with the help, conscious or otherwise, of forces claiming to be socialist or even "communist," to confuse the definition of class, to blur class distinctions and to hide class conflicts. This serves to disarm the working class and prepare the way for increasing attacks upon them by their rulers.

As Warren Buffet, a leading member of the capitalist class in the United States, so candidly admits:

> "There's class warfare alright, but it's my class, the rich class, that's making war, and we're winning."

Communists fight against the false consciousness instilled in workers through the capitalists' control of society by seeking to raise the level of class consciousness among their fellow workers.

25. The capitalist system, driven solely by the quest for more profits for the ruling elite, is destroying the natural environment. Desertification, deforestation and climate change -- which have all resulted from various actions aimed at produced profit in the short-term, without regard to the long-term consequences -- are massive problems facing the human species.

On top of this, the most powerful imperialists are now developing weapons which can physically destroy earth several times over!

At the beginning of the 20th Century, the choice facing all of humanity was socialism or barbarism. Today, as capitalism continues its march towards the destruction of the human species and the planet it inhabits, the choice facing humanity is, quite literally, socialism or death.

The Party

1. The modern communist party is not yet another sect declaring allegiance to this or that doctrine, but rather a force which bases itself on the living -- and constantly developing -- scientific communist theory first developed by Karl Marx and Friedrich Engels. The party's theoretical roots lie in our synthesis of the world communist movement, from its beginnings to today, formulated through a thorough analysis of its failures and successes.

The modern communist party 's outlook is summed up by a statement made by Thomas Sankara, a leader of the 1983 revolution in Burkino Faso, who, along with Karl Marx,

Friedrich Engels, V.I. Lenin, Rosa Luxemburg, Ernesto 'Che' Guevara and others stands among the party's political forebears:

> "We are open to all the winds of the will of the peoples and their revolutions, and we study some of the terrible failures that have given rise to tragic violations of human rights. We take from each revolution only its kernel of purity, which forbids us to become slaves to the reality of others."

2. The primary reason for the existence of the modern communist party is to facilitate, as The Communist Manifesto put it, "the forcible overthrow of all existing social conditions," by acting as the most advanced and resolute part of the working class. The organization of our party, and indeed our methods of work, are completely subordinated to this historic task.

Often, organizations become obsessed with 'democracy for the sake of democracy.' But 'democracy' in and of itself in a revolutionary organization is no guarantee of effectiveness. An organization in which every position of significance was chosen by a vote and subject to recall could easily have a completely incorrect outlook. Likewise, an objectively incorrect position could be held by the majority of the members of an organization.

Communism is not an ideal to be achieved, but rather a movement that grows out of the society of today with real, concrete tasks through which the society of tomorrow can be brought about.

The most important factor for the party is not that it is the 'most internally democratic' organization on earth, but that we are correct in our positions, and that our actions help bring about a communist world.

Organization

1. The modern communist party is organized as a revolutionary combat organization, capable on the one hand of avoiding open encounters with an enemy possessing overwhelmingly superior forces which cannot be won, while on the other hand also capable of exploiting that enemy's every weakness.

While constantly preparing for the revolutionary uprising, the party carries out its preparatory work on combat footing, ready to adapt to any sudden changes which may occur.

2. The modern communist party is organized on the basis of organic centralism, which means that adherence to our program and principles takes precedence over everything else.

Organic centralist organization ensures that the party is not directed by the will of individuals, and their opinions, but by the historical and ideological traditions of the world communist movement, and our communist synthesis, forged through a sober analysis of successes and failures of that movement.

This form of organization is organic in that our leadership and outlook are determined by, and arise through the process of fighting for communism itself, and centralist in that our members are but parts of an organic whole, united around a common goal.

Positions in the modern communist party are filled on the basis of what best enables the party to fight for communism. The appointment of a member to a position in the party is not a promotion or privilege, but an assignment of real responsibility.

3. Owing to the creation of a globalized economy by the capitalist system, the fact that the struggle between the working

class and its capitalist rulers is international, and the reality that the ultimate goal of communism can only be achieved after socialist revolutions are victorious internationally, the modern communist party is organized as a worldwide party.

4. The modern communist party is directed by an International Core, forged through the development of the party, with unbreakable organic ties not only to the organization's membership, but also to the working class. This Core, which is strong, quick to react and at the same time flexible, is guided, and guides in turn, through the fusion of party, which is attained on the basis of the constant common activity and struggle of the entire organization.

5. National sections, directed by national cores (which differ from the International Core only in their reach), exist in each country in which the party has a presence. New national sections are chartered by the International Core.

6. The International Core and national cores are entitled, at all times, full access to all information of importance to the party.

7. The International Core and national cores maintain regular internal circulars to assist with the work and ever-increasing organic unity of the party.

8. Locals, subordinate to the national sections to which they belong, exist in geographic areas in which there at least a few members or candidate members of the party (i.e. a section of a city, a small town, a rural area, etc.).

New locals are chartered by the national sections which they will belong to.

Locals which have grown so large that they can no longer hold effective meetings must be divided (for example by neighborhood).

9. Cells, subordinate to the locals to which they belong (or to the national sections to which they belong, if there is no local) exist in workplaces or organizations (i.e. a factory, a mine, a farm, a military unit, a labor union, etc.) in which there at least a few members or candidate members of the party.

New cells are chartered by the locals which they will belong to, or, if no local exists, by the national sections to which they will belong.

Cells which have grown so large that they can no longer hold effective meetings must be divided (for example, by shift, floor, etc.).

10. Fractions, directed by the national sections to which they belong, exist in industries, trade unions and military forces in which the party has multiple cells.

New fractions are chartered by the national sections to which they are to belong.

11. All national sections and fractions should meet as regularly as possible and necessary. Such meetings should be preceded by the maximum level of preparation possible.

12. All locals and cells should hold regular meetings (preferably monthly, bi-weekly or weekly). These meetings should be prepared in advance, to ensure their maximum effectiveness.

13. Whether or not a national section, local, cell or fraction

should operate openly is determined by meticulous examination of the dangers and advantages of its particular situation.

Sections of the party operating underground must protect themselves from discovery and cannot use the same open forms of organization as sections operating openly. Such sections must constantly improve their defensive measures and train their members in methods of underground work.

14. Directives and decisions of the party are binding on each of its sections, and as a matter of course, each individual member. Such directives and decisions must be implemented without delay.

15. When differences of opinion arise as to the correct course of action, a decision must be made beforehand within the party. No member, or members, of the party may publicly take positions which differ from those of the party. The analyses, positions, slogans and overall outlook put forward in our press, leaflets, pamphlets, speeches, etc., and through our other political work, belong to the modern communist party. If a member, or members, feel any or all of these do not correspond with our program and principles, it is their responsibility to struggle within the party to set it on the right track, rather than separating themselves from the party in the interest of 'saving their purity.'

It is the worst breach discipline, and among the worst errors in combat to disrupt, or worse, break the unity of the party.

16. While, upon its creation, the party lacks a presence in much of the world, it aims to utilize the base it does have to extend its reach by exploiting the international situation to, as immediately as possible, construct sections in each part of the world.

Membership

1. The membership of the modern communist party is made up of those workers conscious of their role in society and the need for socialist revolution -- in which the working class overthrows the capitalist rulers and seizes power for itself -- to sweep away all forms of exploitation and oppression. The modern communist party is made up of those workers who are capable of representing their class even before it is able to take power, and who are capable of dealing with the responsibilities and dangers present in the struggle by their class to take power, and reorganize society.

The modern communist party is then made up communists, who fight alongside their fellow workers for their immediate aims -- whether they be economic or political -- while always seeking to connect those struggles with other struggles, and steer all such struggles towards the ultimate goal of socialist revolution by pointing out both the necessity of that goal and the correct line march to its realization.

2. Exploiters have no place in the modern communist party, which is a party of the working class.

Friedrich Engels -- one of the "fathers" of communism -- pointed out that, if they were unable to completely break from their class background, members of the bourgeoisie and petit-bourgeoisie would serve as "falsifying elements" in a communist party.

In a private circulation letter to Germany's Social-Democratic leadership written in 1879, Engels wrote:

"It is an unavoidable phenomenon, well established in the course of development, that people from the ruling class also join the proletariat and supply it with educated elements. This we have already clearly stated in the [Communist] Manifesto. Here, however, two remarks are to be made:

"First, such people, in order to be useful to the proletarian movement, must bring with them really educated elements... [At the time most working people were excluded from even basic education, thus requiring them to rely on elements from the possessing classes to some extent.]

"Second, when such people from other classes join the proletarian movement, the first demand upon them must be that they do not bring with them any remnants of bourgeois, petty-bourgeois, etc., prejudices, but that they irreversibly assimilate the proletarian viewpoint. But those gentlemen, as has been shown, adhere overwhelmingly to petty-bourgeois conceptions. ...in a labor party, they are a falsifying element. If there are grounds which necessitate tolerating them, it is a duty only to tolerate them, to allow them no influence in party leadership, and to keep in mind that a break with them is only a matter of time.

"In any case, the time seems to have come [in 1879!]."

History has proved this analysis true.

In many parties claiming to be communist, members of the petit-bourgeoisie dominate, controlling all functions of the organization and carrying out all mental (i.e. theoretical) work, while working class members do all the manual (i.e. leg) work.

Though the period of the ascendancy of capitalism has

largely come to a close, thus severely limiting the number of people from the possessing classes that will come over to the side of the working class, it does still occur (especially in periods of open class conflict). These individuals should be brought into the circle of influence of the party, but unless they can become an integrated part of the working class, they do not belong in the modern communist party.

Members of exploiting classes sympathetic to the cause of the party can support its work from outside. If and when they are able to completely break from their class backgrounds, these individuals may join the party.

3. Members of the party must become an organic party of it. This requires accepting the program, decisions and rules of the party.

4. After receiving a recommendation by a current member, individuals may apply for membership, in writing, to the appropriate body (i.e. if no cell exists, they apply to the local, if no local exists, they apply to the national core, if no national core exists, they apply to the International Core).

If accepted, all applicants must go through a three month candidacy phase, during which time they must prove themselves, before becoming full members. This candidacy phase can be shortened or waived in special cases by the International Core.

5. Each member of the party must pay a regular sustaining contribution, the rate of which is set according to a pre-established scale.

Any member who does not pay their set sustaining contribution for a period of more than one month ceases to be in good standing in the party. Any member who falls more than three months behind on their sustaining contribution will be expelled from the party.

Each member should also take out subscriptions to party publications.

6. Every member must attend, and participate in the preparatory work necessary to make possible the meetings of the national sections, locals, cells and fractions to which they belong.

7. In their public activity, members of the modern communist party must always conduct themselves as disciplined members of a revolutionary combat organization.

8. It is the duty of every member of the party to defend it at all costs. Any member who forsakes this duty and attacks the party will be treated as an opponent of the modern communist party.

9. Secret correspondence between members of the party, aimed at concealing certain views or plans from the party as a whole, would run counter to unitary nature of the party and therefore is expressly forbidden.

10. Due to the very nature of capitalist society itself, certain inequalities exist between members. While the party works to transform each of its members into the best and most well-rounded working-class militants, some of these inequalities cannot be abolished within the organization.

Not every member of the party is able, for example, to deliver a speech or write for the party press. Because of this, the party implements a practical division of work among its members, which may sometimes mean different members will be given different responsibilities (e.g. press work, agitation in rural areas, agitation among women, etc.).

What is important to the party is that each member does the best they possibly can.

The Party Press

1. The party seeks to publish quality publications (especially periodicals) to serve as tools at the service of the working class in its historic struggle. These publications must constantly be developed and improved by the party.

2. All party publications (i.e. periodicals, pamphlets, books, etc.) must be organic parts of the party, completely in line with its outlook, goals, etc.

3. While the modern communist party seeks to print periodicals applicable to as many workers, and in as many languages as possible (e.g. a main international organ in all major languages, individual organs for each national section and fraction, etc.), it's is ultimately more important for the party to have good periodicals than many periodicals.

4. The publications of the party can never become dependent on the exploiters (e.g. needing their advertising dollars). Instead, they must be dependent on the party and the working class for funding.

5. The goal of the party's publications is not to entertain the public at large, or to be deemed "respectable" by the agents of the petit-bourgeoisie or bourgeoisie. The party's newspapers

must above all promote and look after the interests of working people. They must be the leading educators and agitators of the party.

These publications must collect valuable experiences from the entirety of the work of the party, so that they can be presented in a way that acts as a guide for the continual improvement of the party's work.

6. Each party publication must strive to become a working collective of revolutionary workers, i.e. all of those who write for the paper, edit it, lay it out, print it, circulate it and sell it, collect material for articles (e.g. news clippings, first-hand reports, etc.), distribute it daily, etc.

7. Revolutionaries develop the closest ties with the publications of the party when they must work and make sacrifices for them.

When revolutionaries wield a publication as their weapon, they are inspired to constantly sharpen it to ensure its usefulness.

It is not enough for each member of the party to be an active salesperson and agitator for party publications, they must also be equally useful contributors to them. Every noteworthy incident -- from the mistreatment of a group of workers inside a plant in which a cell operates to a meeting on public transportation -- is to be reported at once to the appropriate publications. Fractions must communicate all important information from the industries and unions they operate in -- especially the activity of the misleaders. Reporting and criticisms made by the party's publications on everyday matters help to demonstrate that the party's intimate understanding of the problems of every day life.

The editorial staff of periodicals of the party should treat all incoming reports from the working class and its organizations with great warmth and affection. They should use such material either as short news items, which give the party's periodicals the character of vital working collectives connected with real life struggles, or to make communist theory comprehensible by connecting it with practical examples in the daily lives of working people. When at all possible, the editorial staff of each periodical should hold office hours at convenient times to allow any worker to visit and make requests, criticisms or contributions, which should themselves be utilized in whatever ways possible.

Editors of the party's publications must participate, on an ongoing basis, in the regular work of the party.

8. The party's periodicals are in their true element when they directly participate in the campaigns led by the party. During periods when the party's work is concentrated on certain campaigns, the party's periodicals must be as well. It is the responsibility of the editors of each periodical to put themselves at the service of current campaigns, and to saturate the party's publications with the relevant content.

9. The party's publications must lead fierce struggles against the capitalist press, with its ignoring of certain facts, "bending of the truth" and outright lies, and the press of those claiming to be socialists, communists or other "friends of workers," which treacherously labor in the interests of the bosses by promoting reformism, concealing class antagonisms., etc. All of this must be done in a principled manner, without falling into petty factional polemics.

All members and sections of the party must continually defend the party's publications against their enemies among the exploiters and their allies.

10. Each of the party's periodicals can be maintained only by heavy, ongoing material and financial sacrifices. The means for their expansion and improvement will have to be constantly supplied from the individual members of the party until they ultimately attain wide enough circulation and support that they begin to serve as material support for the party.

11. Sales of subscriptions to the party's publications must be carried out on a regular, systematic basis.

The party must take advantage of every political or social event of importance and every situation in which there is increased motion among the working class.

After every struggle, such as a strike, during which one of the party's periodicals energetically represented the interests of the workers involved, a subscription drive should be launched. Through such a campaign, the party can approach and establish ties with every worker who took part in the struggle.

The party must not allow any public meeting of workers or demonstration to pass without being there to push its periodicals at the beginning, middle and end.

At all times, regular sales and distributions of the party's periodicals should be carried out in the neighborhoods, factories, unions and other units in which the party operates. This is a prime responsibility of every member and section of the party.

12. The party maintains a main international organ, The Beacon, which is published on a regular basis. The party seeks to increase this periodical's frequency and availability (which includes publishing it in many more languages).

The Party's Activity

1. The party is a living and working school, in which organic links are forged between the various parts of the organization through collective work.

Every member of the modern communist party must devote their time and energy to the party and participate in its work.

2. The main goal of the each national section of the party is to facilitate the revolutionary overthrow of the capitalist ruling class in the country in which it operates, as a part of the fight of the party as a whole, and the working class it emerged from and belongs to, to abolish the world capitalist system and begin the transition to communism.

Accordingly, the activity of the party in the capitalist countries is carried out in a way that makes possible the victory of the working class revolution over the possessing classes.

In the period prior to revolution, the most general task of the party can be summed up as follows: "Prepare for revolution. Educate, agitate, build the party to change the world."

3. The party must seek to find the most effective methods of educating and agitating among the working class, which includes making our materials, slogans, rallying cries, etc., as comprehensible as possible -- even to workers far from being class conscious -- through its work.

At the same time, the party must avoid restricting its materials, slogans, etc., to the limited demands and aspirations of those workers that are currently furthest from becoming class conscious. Instead, the party must use the revolutionary kernel in those demands -- which lies in the underlying class relations from which they ultimately stem -- as a point of departure, then develop the demands in ways that bring the workers raising them closer to the communist outlook.

4. The party must make use of everything and everyone in waging the class struggle by distributing work suitably among its members, supporters and sympathizers, and utilizing this work to constantly come in contact with a wider section of the working class and bring its most militant and advanced elements into the organization.

The party must make sure that all members have work to carry out at all times. The party must also assist all members by directing their work systematically and expertly, and by providing them with precise information about the particular conditions they are to work in.

5. The party distinguishes itself from other parties claiming to be communist or socialist -- which spend their time collecting members, promoting reformism, running in capitalist elections which they cannot win, etc. -- through its continual self-sacrificing participation in all struggles of the working class.

The party must be able to act upon all political and economic crises that emerges from capitalism's own contradictions and take advantage of the opportunities they present to point out the contradiction between the capitalist rulers and the working class, and advance our goals.

6. The party must intervene in all struggles, demonstrations, etc., regardless of their initiators, to prove itself to workers engaged in such struggles and raise the banner of revolution.

Members of the party must prepare for such interventions in advance, and be ready to take part in them with revolutionizing slogans, speeches, materials, etc., which grow out of the concrete life of working people and point the way forward to liberation. The party must become intimately involved in the concrete questions facing working people; it must help fellow workers to find answers to these questions; it must point out every instance of oppression and exploitation; it must help fellow workers develop a spirit of solidarity, helping along the development of class consciousness by continually pointing to the common cause of all working people.

During revolutionary situations, the party can dispense with specific demands and appeal, in basic language, to working people at large to fight for everything they want and need, and to push to the side anything -- including organizations to which they may belong -- that gets in their way.

7. The party will sometimes initiate demonstrations with certain goals in mind (e.g. education, preparation for industrial action, building consciousness, demonstrating the force of the working class, etc.).

The members and sections responsible for such actions must be flexible, dedicated to the aims of the demonstration, and able to discern at any moment whether the demonstration has reached the peak of its effectiveness and should be brought to a close, or can be intensified and expanded into other forms of action.

When the aims of a demonstration that is suppressed continue to generate wider and wider support among the working class, alternate form of action, or a continuance of the demonstration in spite of repression may be required. In any case, abandonment of the struggle at such a crucial juncture must be avoided at all costs.

8. During strikes, lockouts and other mass dismissals of workers, the party must mobilize in force to take part in the struggle. No matter how small the demands of the workers

involved in such a struggle, the party must get involved.

The party does not use the excuse of waiting for the final revolutionary uprising to ignore or oppose any such struggles. Likewise, the party does not blindly instigate pointless strikes and other reckless actions which can be of no benefit to the working class.

The party takes actions which will win it the reputation as the ablest of working class forces in the struggle.

Locals, cells and fractions must make use of all the ties they have developed among workers when they go on strike. If no ties have been made with striking workers, the opportunity provided by the strike itself must be taken advantage of.

Members and sections of the party operating in the areas and industries in which a strike occurs should organize strike meetings in which carefully formulated communist slogans, strategies and tactics -- which show the workers in question the way out of their plight -- must be raised. If the party is not strong enough to hold strike meetings on its own, it must intervene at meetings called by the union or other forces.

If the resolutions, motions, slogans, etc., put forward by the party at strike meetings are taken up by the majority of striking workers, strenuous efforts must be made to have these resolutions, motions, slogans, etc. taken up at all other meetings connected to the struggle (or struggles) in question.

Resolutions, motions, slogans, etc., which strike a chord with workers engaged in a struggle against the bosses should also be promoted through well placed posters (which can be pasted-up outside of the workplace, outside of bars and restaurants the workers frequent, in major transportation centers like train stations, etc.) and leafleting and individual discussion on the picket lines and more generally. At the same time, sizable sections of relevant party publications, and all members and sections of the party in the area or industry involved, must be dedicated to the campaign being waged.

When bureaucratic strike leaderships cave in prematurely, the party must push for their swift replacement with communist revolutionaries from the party who will act in a firm and resolute manner.

9. Besides participating in the struggles of their fellow workers, members of the party must continually educate and agitate through individual discussions (e.g. going door to door, talking to fellow workers on the job, etc.) and distributing the party's publications.

Members of the party in large cities should carry out organized street agitation whenever possible, and tie it in with leaflet/publication distribution and the placing of posters and stickers.

10. Cells and fractions must carry out regular agitation on an individual level (e.g. conversations with fellow workers on breaks, before union meetings, etc.) and distribute the party's literature.

Locals operating in the same areas should participate in this work by agitating outside of the workplace (e.g. selling newspapers outside a factory in which a cell is operating).

11. Cells and fractions operating inside of labor unions must not simply repeat the general principles of communism and the party, rather, they must formulate a response to each question that arises through their communist outlook and understanding.

For example, instead of opposing every wage agreement on the basis that no matter the pay, workers are still wage slaves, a fraction should fight against the actual content of wage agreements advocated by sell-out union leaders. The fraction could wage such a fight by pointing out the intentions of the sell-out union tops, who seek to preserve their own positions while appeasing the capitalist bosses and smashing class consciousness, and by advancing agreement proposals which go directly against these intentions and are in the interests of the workers.

12. An important part of the work of cells and fractions, and the party more generally, is the struggle against union leaders and other misleaders which claim to represent workers while they are in bed with the bosses.

The party has no illusions in any possibilities of persuading such misleaders and sellouts, and organizes the struggle against them with the utmost energy. The only sure way to carry out such a struggle is to split away workers who support them by exposing such individuals as the traitors and lackeys of the bosses that they are, which includes, whenever possible, putting them in situations that force them to reveal their true colors. Even when this is not possible, the very words and actions of the misleaders and sell-outs can be dissected and offered up as proof of their unreliability and traitorous nature.

A struggle must also be waged against low-level union bureaucrats who defend their actions by hiding behind official rules, "binding agreements" and orders from higher-ups, either out of weakness or aspirations to become high-level bureaucrats themselves. These individuals must be forced to declare openly, and prove through their actions, whether they stand with the bosses or the rank-and-file workers.

During open conflict with the bosses (e.g. strikes, lockouts, etc.), the party joins and pushes forward the most militant workers, thus helping to expose the conservative union bureaucrats who oppose all direct confrontations.

13. Cells and fractions must participate in union meetings and conferences to advance their goals. This requires serious advance preparation, so that these sections can present their

own resolutions and speakers to present and support motions, nominate capable and experienced comrades from election, etc.

14. Sections of the party hold open meetings, study circles, movie showings, and other similar events in the course of their work.

To ensure that they are utilized to their maximum potential, these events must be carefully prepared in advance by all sections of the party involved.

15. The party must do all that it can to continually draw unorganized workers, who are devoid of class consciousness, into its sphere of influence. A major part of this work consists of inducing these fellow workers to join labor unions and read the party's publications.

16. Members and sections of the modern communist party must utilize associations in which workers participate (such as sports and athletic clubs, organizations of war victims and veterans, organizations of retirees and pensioners, etc.) to help expand the reach of the party.

The party may also create such organizations, or other similar organizations (e.g. youth and women's organizations, farm workers' associations, etc.) with the same goal in mind (for more on this see the section entitled Affiliated and Independent Organizations).

17. In rural areas, sections of the party must agitate door-to-door, reaching all individuals' homes in the areas of their work.

18. Of special importance when dealing with poor peasants,

small family farmers, and other semi-proletarian elements in rural areas is giving assistance to such forces to help them overcome small difficulties, drawing them to free educational meetings and exposing their natural enemies (i.e. the bankers, landlords, etc.) as representatives and personifications of the capitalist system as a whole.

19. The party is not pacifistic in its opposition to the militaries of the capitalist states. While the party combats the military institutions of the capitalist state and the capitalist rulers in general with all of its might, it also utilizes institutions such as rifle clubs, the army, etc., for the training they give to working people, which can be utilized in revolutionary battles.

The party opposes all forms of gun control and argues that every possibility for the working class to get weapons, and training in the use of those weapons, must be utilized.

Members of the party do not volunteer for capitalist armies, but will join their working class brothers and sisters in arms if they are drafted, all the time working to educate and agitate among their fellow soldiers and sailors.

Individual members and cells operating within military units (e.g. platoon, squad, etc.), and fractions operating within military branches (e.g. army, navy, etc.), carry out varying types of work depending on the specific conditions they face.

Of primary importance is making fellow rank-and-file soldiers aware of the obvious class division evident in the privileges enjoyed by the officers and the harsh treatment of the ranks, as well as convincing them of the reality that their future in inextricably tied up with the fate of the working class.

During the advanced period characterized by incipient revolutionary ferment (e.g. mutiny, mass refusal to deploy, etc.), and the revolutionary outbreak itself, the party agitates for the democratic election of all officers by the soldiers and sailors and for the formation of democratic soldiers councils.

20. The party opposes -- with all the force it can muster -- the special class-war shock-troops of the capitalist rulers. When these bodies are made up largely of individuals from working class backgrounds, the party combats them until that time when the disintegration of their ranks can be successfully promoted. Those bodies having a homogeneous class character, such as those whose ranks are drawn purely from the officer corps, must be exposed for their every criminal action, so that they become so hated and isolated from the entire population that they eventually break down from within.

21. In countries in which national minorities / oppressed nations form a part of the population, special attention must be given to carrying out education and agitation among their working class sections. In some cases, it may be necessary to create special publications for this purpose.

Special attention must also be paid to work among immigrant workers, and in building solidarity between by the immigrant and native-born workers of each country by pointing out their common interests. Contrary to sell-out union tops that condemn immigrant workers for "bringing down wages" and "taking jobs" from native-born workers, the party fights for full equality for all immigrant workers -- by demanding full citizenship for all immigrants everywhere, to raise them up to the level of native-born workers -- so that the bosses cannot rely on them for cheap labor, to replace striking workers, etc.

The party points out that capitalism is international -- that capitalists take their businesses anywhere in the world they want to go, crossing all borders without any "passports" -- while working people are restricted to certain geographic areas marked by artificial borders. The party constantly raises the question, "Why is capital free while workers remain enchained?"

22. The party, and each of its sections, must constantly and systematically educate members in theory and practice.

23. Although it is established fact that the working class cannot take control of the capitalist state and use it for its own purposes (let alone to liberate itself), the party may, at certain times and in certain conditions, stand candidates in "democratic" capitalist elections.

When the party does so it is because either the elections provide a special or unique opportunity to educate and agitate or expose the capitalist system and capitalist "democracy," a unique situation has arisen in which revolutionary candidates have a real chance of being elected (and thus acting as spokespeople of the exploited in the camp of the class enemy), or a combination of the two.

If elected, members of the party speak for the modern communist party and their class in the parliamentary bodies, or in certain cases, refuse to take their seats.

24. The party actively participates in the "culture war" through the creation of workers' media (e.g. television shows, internet videos, cultural magazines, radio programs, etc.), as well as intervention into established media (e.g. letter writing campaigns aimed at capitalist newspapers and television networks, opinion pieces submitted to capitalist newspapers, promotion of the party's outlook and publications through appearances on television and radio shows, etc.).

25. The party conducts social-welfare work, including, but not limited to mass feedings, dinners, disaster relief, raising money for striking workers, etc., in the interests of the working class. This is done to reinforce and establish new organic ties with a continually widening section of the working class, to

demonstrate to working people that the party acts in their interests and to help bring working people into political life by taking their mind off of their immediate needs (it's hard for a person who is starving to think of anything but food while a person with a full stomach can more easily look at the larger picture).

26. The obligation of all members and sections of the party to do work includes the obligation to report. General reports covering an individual or section's work over short period of time must be made regularly. If assigned a special area of work, an individual or section must report on their progress. Reports should not be limited to the actions of their author/s, but should include all relevant information, including the objective conditions which may have bearing on the struggle.

All reports should filter towards the center. For example, if comrade X belongs to a cell in ABC Steel Works, and is given an assignment by that cell, she must report back to it. That cell should then report back to the local to which it belongs (if applicable). That local should in turn report back to the national core to which it belongs. The national core should finally report back to the International Core.

Reporting must be one of the best traditions of the party.

All reports should be discussed in each of the bodies that they pass through.

Affiliated and Independent Organizations

1. In the course of its work, the modern communist party will undoubtedly find it necessary to develop special organizations for certain areas of work. These organizations may be established as wings of the party, independent organizations subordinate to the party or autonomous organizations.

2. If the party finds it necessary, it may form broad opposition factions (e.g. within a trade union) or have members enter existing ones. In any such bodies, members of the party must seek to gain positions of leadership.

3. The party may also find it necessary, in certain circumstances, to form independent economic associations (e.g. unions). Such associations must never exclude workers who do not accept the outlook, principles, etc., of the party.

About the Author

Ricardo Santiago was an activist working toward the construction of an international socialist network aimed at overturning the global capitalist system of exploitation. He produced numerous written materials in pursuit of that goal.

Over a period of years he wrote on topics ranging from the situation in Korea to revolutions in places like Afghanistan and Nicaragua and strikes in the United States.

Although he began to reconsider some of his positions as the organizations he belonged to collapsed, he never forsook socialism. His writings continue to retain historical, political and intellectual value.

By The Same Author

Socialism and Struggle: Selected Works

Who Will Save The Human Race?

Available through Amazon and by special order through book sellers everywhere.

www.ingramcontent.com/pod-product-compliance
Lightning Source LLC
Chambersburg PA
CBHW070214260726
48658CB00006BA/2075

* 9 7 8 1 7 2 6 3 1 9 3 1 7 *